Clever Comprehension: Book 1

A Guide To Excellent Reading

At Key Stage 2, many children find it challenging to read texts from different genres. In fact, one of the most challenging areas of learning for many children is understand the meaning behind the texts they've read.

It's one thing to read a story and another to understand what it means. The questions in *Clever Comprehension: Book 1* are designed to get students to think about what they've read and to assess their learning.

How can you improve your reading?

The first key to becoming a better reader is to read more. Read for at least ten minutes before you go to bed. Read for ten minutes in the morning and read for at least ten minutes before you watch a TV program or play games. By reading more often, you'll improve your ability to understand more complicated sentences, texts and stories.

Another way to improve your reading and

comprehension skills is to read a wider variety of books. Don't just stick to reading the same type of books all the time. For example, read a book from one genre one week and then another genre another week. In doing so, you'll begin to understand a wider variety of texts and you'll find comprehension exercises to be a lot easier.

I hope these tips have helped you to think of changes that you could make to your reading. Now get started on the following comprehensions and aim to do your best and learn from your mistakes.

If you look at a map of the world, you will see, in the left-hand upper corner of the Eastern Hemisphere, three Islands lying in the sea. They are England and Scotland, and Ireland. England and Scotland form the greater part of these Islands. Ireland is the next in size. The little neighbouring islands, which are so small upon the map as to be mere dots, are chiefly little bits of Scotland, - broken off, I dare say, in the course of a great length of time, by the power of the restless water.

In the old days, a long, long while ago, before Our Saviour was born on earth and lay asleep in a manger, these Islands were in the same place, and the stormy sea roared round them, just as it roars now. But the sea was not alive, then, with great ships and brave sailors, sailing to and from all parts of the world. It was very lonely. The Islands lay solitary, in the great expanse of water. The foaming waves dashed against their cliffs, and the bleak winds blew over their forests; but the winds and waves brought no adventurers to land upon the Islands, and the savage Islanders knew nothing of the rest of the world, and the rest of the world knew nothing of them.

It is supposed that the Phoenicians, who were an ancient people, famous for carrying on trade, came in ships to these Islands, and found that they produced tin and lead; both very useful things, as you know, and both produced to this very hour upon the sea-coast. The most celebrated tin mines in Cornwall are, still, close to the sea. One of them, which I have seen, is so close to it that it is hollowed out underneath the ocean; and the miners say, that in stormy weather, when they are at work down in that deep place, they can hear the noise of the waves thundering above their heads. So, the Phoenicians, coasting about the Islands, would come, without much difficulty, to where the tin and lead were.

The Phoenicians traded with the Islanders for these metals, and gave the Islanders some other useful things in exchange. The Islanders were, at first, poor savages, going almost naked, or only dressed in the rough skins of beasts, and staining their bodies, as other savages do, with coloured earths and the juices of plants. But the Phoenicians, sailing over to the opposite coasts of France and Belgium, and saying to the people there, 'We have been to those white cliffs across the water, which you can see in fine weather, and from that country, which is called Britain, we bring this tin and lead,' tempted some of the French and Belgians to come over also. These people settled themselves on the south coast of England, which is now called Kent; and, although they were a rough people too, they taught the savage Britons some useful arts, and improved that part of the Islands. It is probable that other people came over from Spain to Ireland, and settled there.

Thus, by little and little, strangers became mixed with the Islanders, and the savage Britons grew into a wild, bold people; almost savage, still, especially in the interior of the country away from the sea where the foreign settlers seldom went; but hardy, brave, and strong.

The whole country was covered with forests, and swamps. The greater part of it was very misty and cold. There were no roads, no bridges, no streets, no houses that you would think deserving of the name. A town was nothing but a collection of straw-covered huts, hidden in a thick wood, with a ditch all round, and a low wall, made of mud, or the trunks of trees placed one upon another. The people planted little or no corn, but lived upon the flesh of their flocks and cattle. They made no coins, but used metal rings for money. They were clever in basketwork, as savage people often are; and they could make a coarse kind of cloth, and some very bad earthenware. But in building fortresses they were much more clever.

They made boats of basketwork, covered with the skins of animals, but seldom, if ever, ventured far from the shore.

They made swords, of copper mixed with tin; but, these swords were of an awkward shape, and so soft that a heavy blow would bend one. They made light shields, short pointed daggers, and spears - which they jerked back after they had thrown them at an enemy, by a long strip of leather fastened to the stem. The butt-end was a rattle, to frighten an enemy's horse. The ancient Britons, being divided into as many as thirty or forty tribes, each commanded by its own little king, were constantly fighting with one another, as savage people usually do; and they always fought with these weapons.

They were very fond of horses. The standard of Kent was the picture of a white horse. They could break them in and manage them wonderfully well. Indeed, the horses (of which they had an abundance, though they were rather small) were so well taught in those days, that they can scarcely be said to have improved since; though the men are so much wiser. They understood, and obeyed, every word of command; and would stand still by themselves, in all the din and noise of battle, while their masters went to fight on foot.

The Britons could not have succeeded in their most remarkable art, without the aid of these sensible and trusty animals. The art I mean is the construction and management of war-chariots or cars, for which they have ever been celebrated in history. Each of the best sort of these chariots, not quite breast high in front, and open at the back, contained one man to drive, and two or three others to fight - all standing up. The horses who drew them were so well trained, that they would tear, at full gallop, over the most stony ways, and even through the woods; dashing down their masters' enemies beneath their hoofs, and cutting them to pieces with the blades of swords, or scythes, which were fastened to the wheels, and stretched out beyond the car on each side, for that cruel purpose. In a moment, while at full speed, the horses would stop, at the driver's command. The men within would leap out, deal blows about them with their swords like hail, leap on the horses, on the pole, spring back into the chariots anyhow; and, as soon as they were safe, the horses tore away again.

(An extract from *A Child's History of England by Charles Dickens*)

1. Which three lands can be found to the left, upper corner of the Eastern hemisphere?
(1 mark)

_____

2. What separates the lands from each other?
(2 marks)

_____

_____

_____

3. Who might the narrator be referring to as
'Our Saviour'? (1 mark)

_____

4. In your own words, describe how the land
used to be in previous centuries? (2 marks)

_____

_____

_____

5. What were the Phoenicians famous for producing? (2 marks)

_____

_____

_____

6. What made the Phoenicians special?
(2 marks)

_____

_____

_____

7. In your own words, write a description that compares the differences between the native Islanders and the Phoenicians.   (3 marks)

_____

_____

_____

_____

_____

8. Name one way in which the Phoenicians
changed the way the British behaved. (1 mark)

_____

_____

9. Using the above extract, match the correct
synonyms together: (3 marks)

Misty   Cold

Coarse   Barbaric

Thick   Intellectual

Clever	Unrefined
Savage	Bulky
Awkward	Foggy
Icy	Odd

10. Which form of art was popular amongst the British and why?   (3 marks)

_____

_____

_____

Mark: _____ / 20

The street was small and what is called quiet, but it drove a thriving trade on the weekdays. The inhabitants were all doing well, it seemed, and all emulously hoping to do better still, and laying out the surplus of their gains in coquetry; so that the shop fronts stood along that thoroughfare with an air of invitation, like rows of smiling saleswomen. Even on Sunday, when it veiled its more florid charms and lay comparatively empty of passage, the street shone out in contrast to its dingy neighbourhood, like a fire in a forest; and with its freshly painted shutters, well-polished brasses, and general cleanliness and gaiety of note, instantly caught and pleased the eye of the passenger.

Two doors from one corner, on the left hand going east, the line was broken by the entry of a court; and just at that point, a certain sinister block of building thrust forward its gable on the street. It was two stories high; showed no window, nothing but a door on the lower story and a blind forehead of discoloured wall on the upper; and bore in every feature, the marks of prolonged and sordid negligence. The door, which was equipped with neither bell nor knocker, was blistered and distained. Tramps slouched into the recess and struck matches on the panels; children kept shop upon the steps; the schoolboy had tried his knife on the mouldings; and for close on a generation, no one had appeared to drive away these random visitors or to repair their ravages.

Mr. Enfield and the lawyer were on the other side of the by-street; but when they came abreast of the entry, the former lifted up his cane and pointed.

"Did you ever remark that door?" he asked; and when his companion had replied in the affirmative, "It is connected in my mind," added he, "with a very odd story."

"Indeed?" said Mr. Utterson, with a slight change of voice, "and what was that?"

(An extract from *The Strange Case of Dr Jekyll & Mr. Hyde* by Robert Louis Stevenson)

1. The author states that the street 'drove a thriving trade on all week-days.' In your own words explain what a thriving trade might be. (2 marks)

_____

_____

_____

2. In paragraph two, which four words suggest that the building was neglected? (3 marks)

_____

_____

_____

3. What stood out compared to the
   neighbourhood? (1 mark)

   _____

   _____

4. Identify and write down one simile that is
   used in the extract. Why is this simile
   effective? (4 marks)

   _____

   _____

   _____

5. Which **2** types of people are seen
   surrounding the neglected building?
   (1 mark)

   _____

   _____

6. Many people had tried to drive away the people and ravages. This statement is: (1 mark)

   True   **False**

7. Mr. Enfield and the lawyer are beside the entrance to the building (the door). Which one of them lifts the cane and points? Give a reason for your answer. (3 marks)

   _____

   _____

   _____

Mark: ____ / 15

A fly bit the bare head of a bald man who, endeavouring to destroy it, gave himself a heavy slap.

Escaping, the Fly said mockingly, "You who have wished to revenge, even with death the prick of a tiny insect, see what you have done to yourself to add insult to injury?"

The bald man replied, "I can easily make peace with myself, because I know there was no intention to hurt. But you, an ill-favoured and contemptible insect who delights in sucking human blood, I wish that I could have killed you even if I had incurred a heavier penalty."

(The Bald Man & The Fly: An Aesop's Fable translated by George F. Townsend)

1. Why did the fly bite the bald man?

   (1 mark)

   _____

   _____

_____

_____

2. Why do you think the bald man tried to
    slap the fly? (1 mark)

_____

_____

3. Suggest one reason why the fly tried to
    mock the bald man. Give an explanation
    for your answer. (2 marks)

_____

_____

_____

4. Circle three synonyms that have similar meanings to the word **'contemptible.'** (3 marks)

Friendly   Abject   Ugly   Vile

Intelligent   Wise   Estimable   Ignoble

5. What lesson or moral might readers learn from this story? (3 marks)

_____

_____

_____

Mark: ___ / 10

By the side of a wood, in a country a long way off, ran a fine stream of water; and upon the stream there stood a mill. The miller's house was close by, and the miller, you must know, had a very beautiful daughter.

She was, moreover, very shrewd and clever; and the miller was so proud of her, that he one day told the king of the land, who used to come and hunt in the wood, that his daughter could spin gold out of straw.

Now this king was very fond of money; and when he heard the miller's boast his greediness was raised, and he sent for the girl to be brought before him. Then he led her to a chamber in his palace where there was a great heap of straw, and gave her a spinning-wheel, and said, 'All this must be spun into gold before morning, as you love your life.' It was in vain that the poor maiden said that it was only a silly boast of her father, for that she could do no such thing as spin straw into gold: the chamber door was locked, and she was left alone.

She sat down in one corner of the room, and began to bewail her hard fate; when on a sudden the door opened, and a droll-looking little man hobbled in, and said, 'Good morrow to you, my good lass; what are you weeping for?' 'Alas!' said she, 'I must spin this straw into gold, and I know not how.' 'What will you give me,' said the hobgoblin, 'to do it for you?' 'My necklace,' replied the maiden. He took her at her word, and sat himself down to the wheel, and whistled and sang:

> **'Round about, round about,**
> **Lo and behold!**
> **Reel away, reel away,**
> **Straw into gold!'**

And round about the wheel went merrily; the work was quickly done, and the straw was all spun into gold.

When the king came and saw this, he was greatly astonished and pleased; but his heart grew still greedier of gain, and he shut up the poor miller's daughter again with a fresh task. Then she knew not what to do, and sat down once more to weep; but the dwarf soon opened the door, and said, 'What will you give me to do your task?' 'The ring on my finger,' said she. So her little friend took the ring, and began to *work at the wheel again, and whistled and sang:*

> **'Round about, round about,**
> **Lo and behold!**
> **Reel away, reel away,**
> **Straw into gold!'**

Till, long before morning, all was done again.

The king was greatly delighted to see all this glittering treasure; but still he had not enough: so he took the miller's daughter to a yet larger heap, and said, 'All this must be spun tonight; and if it is, you shall be my queen.'

As soon as she was alone that dwarf came in, and said, 'What will you give me to spin gold for you this third time?' 'I have nothing left,' said she. 'Then say you will give me,' said the little man, 'the first little child that you may have when you are queen.' 'That may never be,' thought the miller's daughter: and as she knew no other way to get her task done, she said she would do what he asked. Round went the wheel again to the old song, and the manikin once more spun the heap into gold.

The king came in the morning, and, finding all he wanted, was forced to keep his word; so he married the miller's daughter, and she really became queen.

(An extract from *Rumpelstiltskin by the Grimm Brothers*)

1. In your own words describe where the story is set. (2 marks)

_____

_____

_____

2. What was near the miller's house?
   (1 mark)

   _____

   _____

3. What might the word **shrewd** mean?
   (1 mark)

   _____

   _____

   _____

4. Which **4 words** would best describe the
   king and why? (4 marks)

   _____

_____

_____

_____

_____

5. Write a description of what you think a
hobgoblin might look like.   (4 marks)

_____

_____

_____

_____

_____

_____

6. Does the king show any sympathy towards the miller's daughter? Explain your answer using evidence from the text. (3 marks)

_____

_____

_____

_____

_____

7. What impressions does the writer give of the miller's daughter? (3 marks)

_____

_____

_____

8. Why did the miller's daughter agree to give her first-born child to the goblin? (2 marks)

_____

_____

_____

Mark: ___ / 20

Nearby a great forest <u>dwelt</u> a poor woodcutter, his wife and his two children. The boy was called Hansel and the girl Gretel.

He had little money and was so <u>destitute</u> that he could not even afford to by a loaf of bread. He thought night and day about how he would feed his family and groaned to his wife: 'what is to become of us? How are we to feed our poor children, when we no longer have anything even for ourselves?' 'I'll tell you what, husband,' answered the woman, 'early tomorrow morning we will take the children out into the forest to where it is the thickest; there we will light a fire for them, and give each of them one more piece of bread, and then we will go to our work and leave them alone. They will not find the way home again, and we shall be rid of them.' 'No, wife,' said the man, 'I will not do that; how can I bear to leave my children alone in the forest? The wild animals would soon come and tear them to pieces.' 'Oh, you fool!' said she, 'then we must all four die of hunger, you may as well plane the planks for our coffins,' and she left him no peace until he consented. 'But I feel very sorry for the poor children, all the same,' said the man.

The two children had also not been able to sleep for hunger, and had heard what their stepmother had said to their father. Gretel wept bitter tears, and said to Hansel: 'Now all is over with us.' 'Be quiet, Gretel,' said Hansel, 'do not distress yourself, I will soon find a way to help us.' And when the old folks had fallen asleep, he got up, put on his little coat, opened the door below, and crept outside. The moon shone brightly, and the white pebbles which lay in front of the house glittered like real silver pennies. Hansel stooped and stuffed the little pocket of his coat with as many as he could get in. Then he went back and said to Gretel: 'Be comforted, dear little sister, and sleep in peace, God will not forsake us,' and he lay down again in his bed. When day dawned, but before the sun had risen, the woman came and awoke the two children, saying: 'Get up, you sluggards! We are going into the forest to fetch wood.' She gave each a little piece of bread, and said: 'There is something for your dinner, but do not eat it up before then, for you will get nothing else.' Gretel took the bread under her apron, as Hansel had the pebbles in his pocket. Then they all set out together on the way to the forest. When they had walked a short time, Hansel stood still and peeped back at the house, and did so again and again. His father said: 'Hansel, what are you looking at there and staying behind for? Pay attention, and do not forget how to use your legs.' 'Ah, father,' said Hansel, 'I am looking at my little white cat, which is sitting up on the roof, and wants to say goodbye to me.' The wife said: 'Fool, that is not your little cat, that is the morning sun which is shining on the chimneys.' Hansel, however, had not been looking back at the cat, but had been constantly throwing one of the white pebble-stones out of his pocket on the road.

When they had reached the middle of the forest, the father said: 'Now, children, pile up some wood, and I will light a fire that you may not be cold.' Hansel and Gretel gathered brushwood together, as high as a little hill. The brushwood was lighted, and when the flames were burning very high, the woman said: 'Now, children, lay yourselves down by the fire and rest, we will go into the forest and cut some wood. When we have done, we will come back and fetch you away.'

(An extract from *Hansel & Gretel* by the Brothers Grimm)

1. Explain the meanings of the four words underlined in the text. (2 marks)

_____

_____

_____

2. Why did the step-mum want to abandon the children? (2 marks)

_____

_____

_____

_____

_____

3. Explain the following sentence:

   (2 marks)

"She left him no peace until he consented."

_____

_____

_____

4. What impressions does the writer give
   of Hansel and Gretel? (4 marks)

_____

_____

_____

_____

_____

5. Write down **5 words or phrases** that
   can be used to describe Hansel and
   Gretel's personalities. (5 marks)

_____

_____

_____

6. Why is the word '**sluggards**' used to describe the children? Give an explanation for your answer. (5 marks)

_____

_____

_____

_____

_____

_____

Mark: ___ /20

All children, except one, grow up. They soon know that they will grow up, and the way Wendy knew was this. One day when she was two years old she was playing in a garden, and she plucked another flower and ran with it to her mother. I suppose she must have looked rather delightful, for Mrs. Darling put her hand to her heart and cried, "Oh, why can't you remain like this for ever!" This was all that passed between them on the subject, but henceforth Wendy knew that she must grow up. You always know after you are two. Two is the beginning of the end.

Of course they lived at number 14 and until Wendy came, her mother was the chief one. She was a lovely lady, with a romantic mind and such a sweet mocking mouth. Her romantic mind was like the tiny boxes, one within the other, that come from the puzzling East, however many you discover there is always one more; and her sweet mocking mouth had one kiss on it that Wendy could never get, though there is was, perfectly conspicuous in the right-hand corner.

The way Mr. Darling won her was this: the many gentlemen who had been boys when she was a girl discovered simultaneously that they loved her, and they all ran to her house to propose to her except Mr. Darling, who took a cab and nipped in first, and so he impressed her. He never knew about the box, and in time he gave up trying for the kiss.

Mr. Darling used to boast to Wendy that her mother not only loved him but also respected him. He was one of those deep ones who know about stocks and shares. Of course no one really knows, but he quite seemed to know, and he often said stocks were up and shares were down in a way that would have made any woman respect him.

(An extract from *Peter Pan by J. M. Barrie*)

1. How old was Wendy when she realized that all people grow up? (1 mark)

---

2. What did Wendy do to the flower that she found in the garden? (3 marks)

_____

_____

_____

3. Which quote suggests that Wendy's mother didn't want her to grow up? (2 marks)

_____

_____

_____

4. Why is the phrase **'sweet mocking mouth'** used to describe Wendy's mother? (2 marks)

_____

_____

_____

5. Which simile is used to describe Wendy's
   mother's personality? (2 marks)

_____

_____

_____

6. Why is this simile effective? (1 mark)

_____

_____

_____

7. Find one word that means **clear.** (1 mark)

_____

8. What was Wendy's surname? (1 mark)

_____

9. Why did Mrs. Darling fall in love with Mr.
    Darling? (2 marks)

_____

_____

_____

10. What impressions does the writer give of
    Mr. Darling? (5 marks)

_____

_____

_____

Mark: ___ / 20

1. The three lands were England, Ireland and Scotland.

2. The lands are separated by water

3. Jesus Christ

4. The land can be described as solitary, lonely, separated, unadventurous, expansive and separate from the world.

5. The Phoenicians were famous for producing tin and lead.

6. They were able to obtain tin and lead from the mines without much difficulty.

7. A description worthy of 4 marks should make clear distinctions between the Islanders and Phoenicians. For example: Although both the Phoenicians and Islanders can both be described as 'savages,' the Phoenicians possessed many skills such as mining and art. They differed from the Islanders/British

because of their skills in the fields of trade, mining and art.

8. They taught them skills such as art, which helped them to become 'hardy, brave and strong.'

9.

Misty: Foggy
Coarse: Unrefined
Thick: Bulky
Clever: Intellectual
Savage: Barbaric
Awkward: Odd
Icy: Cold

10. The form of art referred to in the extract is the construction of war chariots. They were popular because war chariots were needed to help transport people and goods using horses.

1. A thriving trade might describe a successful business or enterprise where goods or services are sold. For example a market stall or tradeshow.

2. The words that suggest that the building was neglected include: discoloured, sordid, no window, marks and negligence. A mark should be awarded for two correctly identified words or phrases

3. The street stood out compared to the neighbourhood.

4. "The shop fronts stood along that thoroughfare with an air of invitation, like rows of smiling saleswomen." This simile is effective because it compares how inviting the shop front is with the appeal of smiling sales women. Both the shop front and

saleswomen appear attractively so that they can tempt passers-by and encourage them to be drawn into whatever is being sold.

5. Children and tramps.

6. False; nobody in the village tried to drive the visitors away

7. Mr. Enfield is the one who lifts his cane and points. We know this because the word 'former' means the first whilst the latter means the last.

Paper 3 Answers

1. The fly bit the bald man because he was hungry and wanted to suck his blood.

2. The bald man tried to slap the fly because he wanted to stop the fly from hurting him. Perhaps he wanted the fly to move away.

3. One reason why the fly mocked the man is because he assumed that the man had tried to attack or hurt him. However, the bald man had no intentions of harming the fly, he simply wanted to stop whatever was irritating or harming him.

4. The correct synonyms are abject, estimable and vile.

5. The lesson or moral of the story is that those who do wrong without intending to haven't committed harm or sin. However,

those who intend to do wrong (like the fly did) should be punished or at least made aware of their wrongdoing.

Paper 4 Answers

1. The story is set in a far-away land near the side of a wood.

2. The miller's house was near a mill, which was on top of a stream

3. The word shrewd has several meanings. A mark should be given to any of the following words or phrases:
   - Very intelligent
   - Sharp intelligence
   - Clever
   - Cautious
   - Hard-headed

4. Words that might describe the king could include any of the following and more. Marks should be given if the student clearly explains why they've chosen each word.

   - **Greedy**: because he always hungers for more and is not content with what he has.
   - **Money-hungry** because he constantly tries to obtain more money even though he's probably very wealthy.

- **Naïve** because he believes what the miller tells him even though there's no proof that the miller's daughter can turn straw into gold.
- **Malicious** because he locks the miller's daughter in a chamber just so she can produce gold for him.
- **Cold** because he comes across as being uncaring and impersonal. He has no regard for other people's feelings and shows no remorse.

5. A detailed description should contain a clear explanation of what the goblin might look like. A very good description will include a mix of grammatical expressions such as adjectives, adverbs, similes and/or metaphors.

6. A good answer should provide an answer and an explanation that is supported by the text. For example, a

quotation from the story or brief reference to the text.

7. The writer gives the impression that the miller's daughter is fearful of the king. She seems to be powerless and therefore gives into his demands because he is more powerful than her. She doesn't come across as being particularly brave.

8. The miller's daughter agreed to give her first-born to the goblin because she was in a desperate situation and had nothing else to give him in exchange for turning straw into gold. She probably thought that she would find some way out of the situation by eventually breaking the promise to the hobgoblin.

1. **Dwelt:** To live in a specific place or to think, speak or write for about something

   Destitute: To lack necessities, to not have necessitates, to be without something, poverty.

   Consented: to give permission for something to happen, to agree to something or to agree to do something.

   Forsake: to abandon, to give up something, to neglect something or someone.

2. The step-mum wanted to abandon the children because she and her husband were too poor to look after them.

3. The phrase: "She left him no peace until he consented" means that she (the step-mother) wouldn't stop until he listened to her and gave in.

4. The writer gives the impression that Hansel and Gretel are two poor children who have suffered miserably at the hands of their evil parents. The writer gives the impression that Gretel is very emotional but Hansel however, is smart and quick thinking. He therefore comes up with a plan that will save their lives.

5. Words that might describe Hansel & Gretel's personality could include: smart, brave, clever, caring, selfless, loving, and courageous.

6. The word 'sluggard' means lazy but it can also mean slow. The stepmother uses it to describe the children because in her mind, they are a burden to her and her husband. She believes the children are 'sluggards'

because they have not woken up on their
own.

Paper 6 Answers

1. Wendy was two years of age when she learnt that all people grow up.

2. Wendy plucked the flower and gave it to her mother.

3. The quote that suggests that her mother doesn't want her to grow up is: "Oh, why can't you remain like this for ever!"

4. The phrase "sweet mocking mouth" is used to describe Wendy's mother because she says things that on the surface seem to be nice but actually taunt people. For example, she is able to make insults seem like compliments even though they are not.

5. The simile that describes her personality is: "Her romantic mind was like the tiny boxes, one within the other."

6. This simile is effective because it creates an image in the mind of the reader. The image suggests that when it comes to love, her mind is divided into little pieces. The pieces seem different but they fit into each other (like boxes). The simile is therefore effective because it suggests that Wendy's mother is a complicated person who doesn't think in the way that most people do.

7. The word that means clear is 'conspicuous.'

8. Darling

9. Mrs. Darling fell in love with Mr. Darling for several reasons: he didn't try to kiss her, he was intelligent, knew about 'stocks and shares,' and she respected him.

10.   The writer gives the impression that Mr. Darling is a smart and intelligent man. However, we also get the impression that he is slightly arrogant because he 'boasts' by telling Wendy how he impressed her mother.

Texts

- Charles Dickens, *A Child's History of England.*

- Robert Louis Stevenson, *The Strange Case of Dr. Jekyll & Mr. Hyde.*

- Aesop, *The Bald Man & The Fly*

- The Brothers Grimm, *Rumpelstiltskin*

- The Brothers Grimm, *Hansel & Gretel*

- J. M. Barry, *Peter Pan.*

Clever Comprehension: Key Stage 2 Reading Practice 2012.

For more information visit **thetutoress.com**

Printed in Great Britain
by Amazon.co.uk, Ltd.,
Marston Gate.